CHRIS EMERY was born in Manchester in 1963 and became an Irish citizen in 2023. He has published four collections of poetry, a writer's guide, an anthology of art and poems, and edited selections of Emily Brontë, John Keats and Christina Rossetti. He works in publishing and lives in Cromer, North Norfolk. *Wonder* is his fifth collection of poetry.

ALSO BY CHRIS EMERY

POETRY
Dr. Mephisto (2001)
Radio Nostalgia (2006)
The Departure (2012)
Modern Fog (2024)

Chris Emery
Wonder

CROMER

PUBLISHED BY SALT PUBLISHING 2025

2 4 6 8 10 9 7 5 3 1

Copyright © Chris Emery 2025

Chris Emery has asserted his right under the Copyright, Designs and Patents Act 1988 to be identified as the author of this work.

This book is sold subject to the condition that it shall not, by way of trade or otherwise, be lent, resold, hired out, or otherwise circulated without the publisher's prior consent in any form of binding or cover other than that in which it is published and without a similar condition including this condition being imposed on the subsequent publisher.

First published in Great Britain in 2025 by
Salt Publishing Ltd
12 Norwich Road, Cromer, NR27 0AX United Kingdom
www.saltpublishing.com

GPSR representative
Matt Parsons matt.parsons@upi2mbooks.hr
UPI-2M PLUS d.o.o., Medulićeva 20, 10000 Zagreb, Croatia

Salt Publishing Limited Reg. No. 5293401

A CIP catalogue record for this book is available from the British Library

ISBN 978 1 78463 370 7 (Paperback edition)

Typeset in Sabon by Salt Publishing

Printed and bound in Great Britain by Clays Ltd, Elcograf S.p.A

For my mother
MARY JOSEPHINE EMERY née HANRAHAN

and for my father
GERALD EMERY 1929–1981

Contents

Wonder	1
The Berry	2
The Statue	3
You Dream of the Rose God	6
Home Song	7
Leave-Taking	8
Coast Watching	9
On the Forecourt	10
Leonard	11
Sent Here	12
Lust	14
Whit Walks	15
Edith Huntley Makes a Further Stop	16
A Single Ticket to the Imagined City	17
Packing It All In	18
Østerlars	19
Trailer Memories	20
Stitches	21
Twa Tieve's Nackets	22
Levelling Up	23
Im Mozarthaus, Wien	24
The Chaffinch	25
Ochia	26
Bagging Up	28
The Small Life	29
Driving to Carla's	30
The Services	31
Truer	32
Why I'm Calling You	33
Lord of Misrule	34
The Black Abbess	35

The Snow Bed	36
The Arraignment	37
Christmas is Coming	38
The Stone	39
The Blue Afternoon	40
Four Portraits of a Murder	41
History Lessons	42
War Games	43
The Crabs	44
It's Here Again	45
Anastasia in Crinolines	46
Meeting at the Hayward	48
My Spell	49
Them Situationals	50
A Bouquet	52
Tidelines	53
A Town Called 'Proverbs'	54
Identity	55
Goodbye, Gifford	56
The Herald	58
Fresh Deliveries	59
Under the Mesas	60
Ring All the Bells	61
Minor Comedy	62
How Small We Were	64
Jackson's Brick Works	65
The Comeuppance	66
Folk Tale	67
My Idea of Heaven	68
Acknowledgements	69

> [19] 'And I will show wonders in the heavens above
> and signs on the earth below,
> blood, and fire, and vapour of smoke;
> [20] the sun shall be turned to darkness
> and the moon to blood . . .'
>
> Acts 2

> 'I wonder, my little darling,
> where can you be again tonight,
> while the moon is shining bright?
>   I wonder.
>
> 'My heart is aching, why for you
> can our love be mistaken?
> Darling, don't you say that this must mean
> our ending.
>   I wonder.'
>
> PVT. CECIL GANT, 'I Wonder'

> 'The World resembled His *Eternitie*,
>   In which my Soul did Walk;
> And evry Thing that I did see
>   Did with me talk.'
>
> THOMAS TRAHERNE, 'Wonder'

Wonder

But what happens when a rook dies?
Its last attempt at soaring like a dishcloth – perhaps it flies
out into the sweet stripes of dawn
by the edge of town.

Does their jobbing family recover it and each agree
to take up one memory
and keep it
safe and fold it back into the meadow here and sit

high on split oaks grieving, croaking about
seeds and stones,
weeds and bones?
I bet they each turn all their feathers into a primal coat

of darkness close to wonder.
It makes you think how their gathered minds can ponder
the god of hard winter now. They seem to know
the first hint of barley, the lapsing of the snow.

The Berry

When you reach in for this deep berry
alone in sloes and blackthorn
on a dull day of scary
weather, you'll scorn

each year of surrogate daylight the blackbird
stops, all blunt desire
gathering you in empty-handed when you're heard
in pissy grasses leaning through entire

years of thorn clumps, catching
your wrists it takes so long
to pick it, that now you are crying,
placing the fruit on the back of your tongue.

The Statue

You can reach him from the high brick towns
selling fifth-hand carpets or that religion
of furniture near prayer-hoarded townhouses
the trams don't reach. It's a pig sty

beneath those tower blocks
no one remembers being built, then on
through clichés of terracing
and blurred horizons

accelerating in towards the pointy buildings
at the centre; it's all modern there.
Yet his legacy is clearly housed in all those sixties
movies of 'The North' – the awful accents

almost modish then, where
a backdrop foams with river filth
and the busy wives are shawled with
several kinds of misery and he's

stamping his shoes on bare boards.
It's almost always *him* the film
revolves on: a bad suit, a bit of rough,
who makes eight hours of crappy stuff

in a shadowless factory. Then we cut
to piled hairstyles dying through
a montage of cavernous dance halls,
not needed.
                    Dropping down by bingo halls

you're in the centre now, and take a sudden right
to nestle in beside the crippled stacks
with sundial waste around them:
car parks pricing local absences

for the very few who work here. And arriving
at the nether-edge, near the prison or
station or that rectilinear warehouse
partially lettered over gravel bins, you turn

towards a wharf and its rendered dark
of corbels and buttresses showing that sudden
claggy soot no one's cleaned for years.
Slipping into neutral, you settle in

to this older dismal district the shoppers
avoid or race through in the city rain.
If you turn your head from all the dirty bits
and walk along the unfenced

artery of the canal, the dead divide
beneath you in their penultimate academies –
nothing but the sewers dream on,
the rivers are sewn back underground

and black clouds from black towns send
their wet truths over all these new accents
of our separate histories.
There are no victories of common purpose.

And turning left, he's there, the one I meant,
a portly figure no one sees or recognises
in his bronze assumption, laughable above
the fly-posters. I guess he made it here.

You Dream of the Rose God

Do you think the night matters?
The rose god steps one way
then another through the dumb map of you.

You recall trucks in a blue desert;
hanging trees in a white apartment;
parapets and green lakes; birds in the cage.

I'm not sure the scale of it can hold us:
each gesture we make
furthering the dark.

All we love filling
the swift hands of the rose god
counting and counting all his sand.

Home Song

Let's find a wet path to the river
and clap to the finch's rain song
and hear the hidden raven bark

all its three-time news for us
beside the ruined umber water.
You can have this life today, I know,

and give me never-ending rain,
iron-black houses, soot-grey dawn,
the love of other weather, only

set me on this wet path to the river,
by the last imperial city filled
with musk mallow and ragged robin.

Leave-Taking

They say, if you stay anywhere long enough
the world will leave.

The common path is rough
it's not as if we fail to see it coming, if

all we chide and cherish passes:
flaming house, moon's adjournment, by and by one kiss,

counterculture silting up young lips,
fingers on a thigh, the apple and its pips,

love leaves no foment in the eye.
Stay anywhere long enough, a world will die.

The dust of what is left descants
on the sore deal absence makes for us.

No world can bear its advocate,
but do not let the world's abeyance grate

beside all the gold-barrelled attractions,
what was always there beside you thins

and we are here to sort the bright-faced gods
of our leave-taking, and pile the sods.

Coast Watching

Later, I tire of the sea, and you say, No.
No, it must be right to fear what's loose,
something bringing mad fog close

or reaching winter lather in the dark.
Folds of sugar kelp in dead seals;
weedy cavities in dead gulls; the sorrow

of each provincial harbour. I stare back,
zip my coat, smile and say I know,
then drag my heels through comb weed.

Like this, the island's fiscal future passes
us forever. It cannot matter
any of us knows these waves will sweep

and perish, diminishing each dark battery.
Each of us is bound to each in care of it.
We turn and watch the white caps breed.

I say it is exhausting to see how late
life is in tides; you laugh at me and say
it is commensurate. The sea in us is time.

On the Forecourt

Out on spec, between two pubs, the van plays up.
That light comes on. I stop for fuel and patches
at that place up by Joe's flat: cranes and hoardings,
lane closures on the inner ring road, it's a joke.
I see myself reflected in the masked-out mini-mart
and feel a breeze turn animal on the forecourt.
You need to stretch your arse to see the numbers
on those pumps. I sense some angled half-lit rain
will soak me as I pay. What does it really say
to understand lost hours in places made like this?
Signs and dump bins, racks of sagging newsprint.
Stuff you never need, until you do. The wasted
unreturning hours shaved from your life that tells
you all you ever meant was never meant to be.

Leonard

When they rinsed down the grey mare, Leonard cried;
when they fetched half-ton pigs from the top field
or last year's rams and ewes from the barrow,
he'd find the need to scour the dairy, mow,
or check the Red Polls were all eating well.
But now, he jabs cold coals. Scrapes an anvil.

They say he can sit by the forge today,
or fix that dry stoning later, but see
to leave the mess to them. No one should pay
for the error of their birth. Nothing's free.
They bring up ropes and harness two old bays
and never once look Leonard in the face.

Legs strapped under tarpaulins, the cart leaks
as they make off. The grim load sways and creaks.
Rooks start their evening service. Elms expire.
Leonard twists a whale oil lamp, lights a fire
crouching under horse brasses in bright rows
just like pappy did, then burns all he knows.

Sent Here
for Matthew Sweeney

I

Just there he shuffled on a coir mat
to hear Latin octets, the song tangled
in grey air, smudged with motes in
an imperial dome, devoid of seats,
working the magisterium into a far
gold herd, its anxiety piped in.

II

Where widows totter in black muslin
this bend of wafer-taut light mixes money
and decay with bitumen and suddenly
the marble spread openly beaches you
under impossible lacquer, waiting
for massed coughing to abate.

III

We all move on to his wake like fools.
Languid shadows, distant radios
and neighbours murmuring of chaos.
Fig rolls, ham and lettuce platters
where oak-demoted rain sags
at horseless lane ends.

IV

And did we find he left us there? Moving on
from shattered frame to frame,
tilting out on one dependable balcony,
watching the empty birds collapsing
over the Hauptfriedhof and counting
steps from the last aborted tram?

Lust

You ask me once again between
cold beers in the corral:
we need to understand them,
the sunsets. It's not that their
shimmer decays with our neighbours
where the young days fall
but we should learn if they die
forever on a curve, fried
on the Earth like us, I mean,
luscious with all this tumult
beyond the last lemon and peach
apartments on a cactus ridge
out beyond blue county lights
suffering the distance
that may never end . . .
                        Still,
I was thinking we should chase
these hours across the final pools
and patios of silent ranches
under this single evening star
that made its home by
the moon's heel this month.
She brings us nothing but
poor weather in bad movies
and learns the sunsets, too.
Making her fertile sign in a smoky
cobalt sky that I beseech you
to call lust.

Whit Walks

A small thing starting out, where all the tribes
still prayed, it spread in weightless childhood
just the same. Whit walks down Broadway, gathered
between posh houses, with all that kept us pure.
Uncomprehending neighbours, gangs and stuff
that needed heeding – from that point on we knew
all the fussy banners in short pants, white shirts,
hair stuck down above clean collars, red ties,
those mandorlas cut out with pinking shears
patched with velvet, lurid on each chest;
walking every symbol and attainment
along the car-less road to make something
utterly a past. And that was that, you know,
another thing that ended with you in it.

Anyway, look at all these Kodak snaps –
the shawls and Sunday best, horn-rimmed glasses,
suits kept for the bookies, a funeral
or Oldham Wakes – adults almost smiling,
old at forty. The dads are bald and dumpy,
the mums all fusty and particular
behind prams that look like boats. All the kids
are staring back at teachers or the priest,
hoping there'll be pop and muffins later.
It's simpler there, for sure, behind the band.
But take your time to check all the little
faces (understanding this was you)
and learn what's gathered there has left no trace:
the common dream we needed to be us.

Edith Huntley Makes a Further Stop

On the River Bure, gold-chambered evening lifts.
Ruptured magenta. Birds in tides. Membered trees.
I consider the lost moorings in my life like this.

Frozen on a farm squatting with autumn turnips
when suicide became the farthest of my hells.
Lying naked in a valley under distant bells

after sex had pushed her treacle-heavy hands
into my womb. The ward in St Andrew's, once again,
when all my days were nameless as the child.

A final letter filled with sins, and misaddressed by her,
that reached me in Bickley; I opened it alone.
And now the hooking years that I look back on:

crêpe bunting, fêtes, black cake tins in stacks.
I have the albums in a dresser.
                          On the staithe, a warm
day relents its filthy flowers – the wasps have come,

the garden is a mirror. I smell the musk of nettles
under oak trees and pause to hear high catching cries
as dark skies fold with darker lines of geese.

A Single Ticket to the Imagined City

When you alight from the grunting 35, turn right
by Jeans Emporium and Pannick's Heel Bar
to note the post-colonial shadows. Forget the map
and head out through the lot, its cinders glinting,
you'll see a circle of fag butts betray the bay
where Jez parked up last night to staunch his wound,
to work things out, who made the call to Pauline
about Roscoe and the dogs before another day of debts.
You'll tread right through the ghost of his Sierra
beside sooty Edwardian shops of offcuts
and remnants hanging on – the inconclusive
family consortium Ajay thought would beat the rot.
You'll see the windows taped with foolscap sheets
that spell out EVRYTHIN MST GO. It went. We all went
with the garment trade to hit the threadbare city.
We are its trade. You'll skirt by Shipton's Market
with its mural of cross-eyed cartoon cats
and once you see the redbrick midtown courts
please stop and wait, for I'll be heading there to meet you,
an older shade that never left, pinned to the spot
you never needed. I'll serve you up a paradise.

Packing It All In

Packing dresses, wondering
how other people do it, pressing in
six balled-up socks, tucking
knickers in three corners,

you catch a glimpse of sunlight
falling like postcards
on a dresser, and concern
yourself with leaving.

Which life shall be razed today
its dust like a marinade?
The half-screwed futon is unmade,
you catch your toes on that.

One ticket proffers another ordinary
place to sigh instead of weeping.
The life you loaned out uselessly
isn't worth keeping.

And what comes next fitfully
creeps west towards loneliness
with such unfashionable cases
to haul through stages

of this giddy journey back to where?
Packing comes to seem
the final test of no affection,
there should be lessons in it.

Østerlars

Smoothing one slack film of hair, he shares his
'anecdote'. We drop our eyes and freeze.
The one in Greece again: him on his knees
sailing the Saronic Gulf, the hell
of Athens over – in love and, yes, self-made –
he lists the bits that we have come to loathe:
sardines with Petros, that taverna, both
scratchy heat and blue eternal shade,
and then the telegram we doubt –

                                        some uncle
ill with something nineteenth-century
asking him to travel on his bursary
to care for him in Bornholm. If looks could kill.
He'll stop in Koszalin and cruise the bars.
We grin and count the miles to Østerlars.

Trailer Memories

For example, Papa Howie's Esterbrook I cherished
but had no ink to use its nib; I never wrote him.
Or the Timex from Bisbee Lula bought me on a bender
along with a crimping iron that sparked on bingo nights.
And I still have her cherry ChapStick that I teased out
with tweezers or a pinkie in the glove compartment
of my Pinto, its bitten through with rust out back,
that after Ray and Tina drank all my Michter's
I dropped a Newport in and burned the leatherette.
But chiefly, my okay life in vinyl-covered stacks
down there, and under pages of semi-sticky you'll see
Polaroids of me being me with Lucas in Buckeye.

Stitches

That when you picked those stitches free
to collect each white tick on the ridge
of an ashtray (onyx, no longer used) you teased
your bad needle through the frayed patch

to lift it off and there, its hem giving way,
we saw the weird unbleached pattern
that had kept its colour from what must be
nineteen sixty-three, so fresh we sucked in air

and felt, for a moment, as if our whispered lives
had dipped back through the pristine cloth
to recapture what was lost beside one radio,
one last cigarette, one love that hadn't ended.

Twa Tieve's Nackets

Where you climb this place again in noon shadows
the water gathers and you are stood

by Clock Loch's milky light.
The last stretch shoves and ruptures

and your skin wholly knows its own decay
that here, so totem still

under cheap garments of orange-lilac cloud
all that is cold and colder by inches

is weather in the rocks. But anyway,
in that place under all the final places

you may hear its grief call bending
and squinny to find the lost one in columnar dark

or still loch pewter
when you spot its sweet tuft and suck your teeth to know

it is the frozen body of the first one yearning
when the second one cries with all that can be empty

and accompanied by what is empty still.
It makes the world exhume its ash creatures that

departing from it shortly, you know the missing love
inside those cries, for this is always kept.

Levelling Up

Arctic birds: your first and last.
    A screaming match you run right past.
A black shale beach and black tide sifting,
a lime green hill with deep fog drifting.
    Through some sixty family years
    we fill it up: the town of tears.

Half a street, then half a terrace,
    behind whose nets each ash-white face.
A genuflecting wheelhouse scene
with half-lit miners in between,
    and through the lot we come to see
    the leftovers of you and me.

Im Mozarthaus, Wien

It is a long cure, that's true,
we're here to venerate
the Mozarthaus, Domgasse,
and let love's lathered
page expire. The white
apartment trembles. Soundless
but for heels on boards
can rooms become a ministry?
Spied below dormers
rain splits on the lintels of Blutgasse.
It's a day of lost erotic light
where huddled crowds subside
in an afternoon of silhouettes.

Here and there, the hollow space
permits its mid-life tourists
to neglect their craving
to defect. In here, we grieve
and point towards panels
whose trompe-l'œil lines
show all that can be lost.
Lemon light ladles
absence after absence
in a comic drill of decency
where each of us suspires.
Square-shouldered, pin-legged,
we lurch through the silences,
notes without a stave.

The Chaffinch

At first, you couldn't really hear it,
the urgent edge each note sent out
below heavy-breathing daybreak
and these mad deliveries being made
in gravel-barrel districts
elsewhere ending someone's shift –
and in the care home someone coughing
across steeply bundled darkness
when finally, the notes work out
above those sporting auburn roofs
to land beside you fully formed:
the freight of childhood working loose,
the wheedled notes the night ship makes
and wet backyards unclenching
in the rain song of the chaffinch.

Ochia
for Jennifer

I know I could charm you with it,
  this cat snake or whip snake
    pointing east in the clay, and you ask
      Is it okay? Is it dead? and I say how scooters
     will miss it here, flat in the silt and it is
    safe for the cure of summer,
    sunning with whatever lies unseen,
    just take this speeding mother, intent
   on driving to the hospital to bear
  the truth like a seventh wound
and where Vasilis is laid out from his spill
  on that rusty Vespa. Yet Cora is with him
    in her torn skirt, her short skirt, explaining
    in heavy gasps, waving her palms,
      that he had leaned out too far
        and there were stones
        where the 'seasonals' double park
      between shifts, the red earth crumbling
    and she talks about this snake,
this *ochia*, that stretched out
beside them where they lay hoping for
one last car from the mountains,
  the snake a silent love mark.
    She says it looked for all the world
    like a jacquard scarf Maya gave her
      for her 'formal' last year and we know,
        this late in blue declining skies, we know
        that it is safe there still, this *ochia*,

Οχιά – pronounced 'oh-hee-ah', a generic name for vipers in Crete.

   as the boy wakes up coughing
     between mother and lover and grins
  so widely when Cora bends in
to share something we cannot hear.
And bites his ear.

Bagging Up

When I scrape your hair from this Kent brush
to form a sort of airy mouse,
I roll it tighter in my palms, then bag it
with other trimmings from the dresser
and this is said to form your ghost.

And when I run my fingers over screeds
of pastel shirts from Guys 'n' Dolls
and yank them awkwardly from hangers,
sorting them for Marie Curie later,
I find the chequered cuffs have frayed,

the fronts are stained with latent meals
from northern carveries or that place
on the moors that served my first Cinzano.
I squash the bin bags flat, then watch them
bloat and breathe with all that's left of you.

The Small Life

Mother said, 'Learn to love a small life,'
between these weak rivers, ruptured fields
where grey sheep fill the view of St Mary's.
A life that hands you down its silty
pea field with that fence no one can mend,
and livestock that won't cost too much.
The virtues of a small life, mother insisted,
ought to involve a diligent tidy marriage
you never managed to supply yourself
and short fat neighbours aplenty,
of whom there are none,

a loyal sheepdog called Thaxton
you never bought from Kenning's Farm,
and family jinx set down on a hundred sheets
in red boxes you never purchased.
It didn't happen, the small life,
but love it still, you do, as Mother wanted.
Now you sit on a blind porch at midnight
with a tiny roll-up that flakes and falls
in your brandy, in the tin cup Mother left,
so full of flies you cannot drink it.

Driving to Carla's

It is a long drive with Ida. Rain tours the dead county.
Not real nature out here, it's sad with prefabs
and tarnished farms. We look ahead and see
half of ourselves mirrored in hazel cloud lines.
What are the nameless tiers called where
sometimes we see a gang of pickers squatting
on glistening ridgeways with something heavy
moving slow into the dead county.

What is it you're saying now about Carla?
'Please, she couldn't love anyone in a proper way.'
I don't reply. Racing to the lonely services
we pass a crossroads with its empty leaning sign,
then a single track on a shaven field that heads out
some place we can never know and wouldn't
want to, really. *'Can anyone do it properly?'*
I stare into the endless east and dream about Carla.

The Services

We stop for a slash and nuggets
and stumble-run through lot winds by
    steel-slat concessions and empty
    steel tables too wet to sit at –

push past vapers and polystyrene swill
to enter the viscous air
    of the atrium: fat queues there.
    Kids dodge warnings of a spill

and 'Hits of the Eighties' pours out
over hissing tin self serves. Someone
    orders farty cartons of meat
    where we see the taupe melamine-

absolute under its arc of
extractor pipes and mauve uplights.
    Is it meant to be a ship? Shites
    by the pastries have a group cough

over the beef slices. A smell
of sugar and piss leaves the old
    looking dour-purgatorial
    by the bogs, where Beatrice is called . . .

Outside, new black weather is tossed.
We grab max packs, fags and Mentos
    and squawk in a jam by the doors.
    All that is loved lives to be lost.

Truer

Knowing nothing of him now except this:
a log of sickness upon sickness
embarrassing to dream. The boatyards west
of reasonable shipping, the wars guessed
at out beyond the jetty. He abstains
from something, shining buttons, but the rains
keep coming far beyond the breakwater.

And if we walk to the same sea later
we'll see something heaving up beside us:
caskets of grey, white-capped, barren and loose,
the way memories are. At least we know,
despite these are not ours, they come to show
something of an appetite for love or
something close to that, not true, but truer.

Why I'm Calling You

Later that morning I begin to scale back
what there is of me – each aspect stripped off
like a wrongly-lettered bra, or some residue on a bus seat,
stories of my blind Aunt's fort, or the anecdote I tell
about the storm-damaged overpass near Smithfield
that carried Rupert's hirsute family
to its grave. *Goodbye, Donna. Hello, Dave.*
Or the time I qualified as a churro cook in Fresno.
I lie about the avenue of horse chestnuts where
Dr Singh taught me the six causes of imperialism,
his kisses tasting of aniseed. He died last summer.
I lie about that horse parade where Toni Dewars
dressed as a gold bear and upskirted Lucille
then threw the Polaroid at me. I have it here.
I appeal to every witness to forget, forget
that time we were eating at La Luz and Amy
choked to death on a fennel seed. So I travel on
through the Chihuahuan Desert to this place called
Gammon, dressed as a priest to help Marcus out,
and I stop off at Lionel's Dry Goods and Electricals
and sit here drinking soda, riffling through
the sagging *Yellow Pages* no one reads anymore;
but I land on the ad for the diamond-coated pangolin,
and that is why I'm calling you.

Lord of Misrule

Lord pimple of the night
I can see the spires of your ears. Whole lemon eyes.
All you eat is liver.

When you said our future was a bloody *semaine*
I imagined us smothering your children with love,
eloping from our wedding to that black edge:

fishy pipe cleaner legs
dashing through the bleach-field among the stones.
No walls. No bandy oaks. All upper dark instead.

Was that our future of heedless stars? The lone lanes?
Why had we demanded this dribbly bed?
That night, we marched a leather outcrop,

fastened corpulent buttonholes
beneath a colander of stars. O yet the flowers wiggled
under an action of moonlight and we yelped.

Months became our tombs, pigs a forest.
Our diary of festooned naval victories
seemed one endless deceitful broth.

Then our signals poured west.
Dear goat, we too are unfinished
dissidents on a final wistful promenade.

The future is all neutrons, you said,
let's dehistoricise the mutton butties.
Everything now has come to this.

The Black Abbess

She's black as tourmaline or burned sugar.
Black as that Saxon spelt loaf they found
eight winters back in a clay pit out here.
In one hand she holds her molten heart
that never found a life with children.
Widowed too, she wasn't bothered
by crusades and deserts. Yet it was him
her prayers poured out to by the hares and eels.
She became the founding abbess here,
or some place close, we can't be sure.
A mason carved her full of vacant pain
then tied her to a cart with hemp ropes
and beat his draught horse to fetch her.

The Snow Bed

The hour before dawn I spend with you
is soot winds, chalk dreams, a scurf of dew,

early traffic adjusting the almost silent house
with its backdoor latch undone, we must not rouse

the children from nylon sheets to see how new
the first hour is when made so blue

or to witness this missing trail, jaunty and inchoate,
in arrow prints from the blackbird's feet

tracing what for us is still impeded here below
in the foreign bed of all this city snow.

The Arraignment

Our dog spotted him in the understory,
lopsided, beak gaping, flapping in the heat.
We wiped our brows and twisted through
broken fencing and nettle clumps to reach him.
His wings still worked short hops in the ferns
but couldn't lift him any higher through field maples.
I shuffled, stooped awkwardly, bolted
and then had him gently, frail as a ball of leaves,
all angle-eyed and sharp and bright minded.
Nothing damaged or bitten through.
I cupped him and looked hard for what was wrong
and he looked back through my skull, just the same,
judging the interruption of the end
or seeing something in me, another fault.

Christmas is Coming

Our dreams are made upon this ship:
400 metres of red containers twist on deck,
its webcams show half-lit floors;
no one moves through any doors.

Slow miles. Iodine. Grey études.
Two chefs in whites broil lamb and beef
to feed the midnight crew
who never loved, who never knew.

One full moon and planets mid-Atlantic.
Sea lanes galvanise the captain's sober years.
A seaman FaceTimes his leukaemic sister.
A seaman pierces a blister.

All our stowed Christmases are grinding
towards Felixstowe or Immingham
through colossal bronze dawns:
a ship with nitrates for our lawns,

crazy plastics or rah-rah skirts –
the things that truly matter –
stowed in this floating church for us.
This is the ship of human urges

and we are its surface for things,
practising each sort of happiness
watching for a simple eastern star
and paradise from China.

The Stone

I found this stone
and kept it.
A lip in the dirt.
Brute jewel –
its knuckle is
cool and dark
and frank
with time.
When I lift it
to pass between
my tired hands
its weight is the weight
of chance,
its colour
is lilac of grief.

The Blue Afternoon

We play chess in the courtyard
bored of the afternoon phantoms.
Tired bees fall. How shall we escape?

Short angles of sunlight fail to pierce us.
We drop like sheets in a famished dream.
Mint tea is served, and we begin our stories.

In this one a deep girl is eating dates,
she finds love in a flaking cobalt atrium.
Lemon trees, parrots and old cats.

Heat wades through the stonework now.
What will become of our sweet child?
Far across the yellow hills the grey wolves turn.

Four Portraits of a Murder

Blanket-stitched flower sacks from Ged Kavanagh's
and this fringed grey hat and jute jacket with torn pockets,
my feet sinking slowly in a queasy paddock
where I'll kill the last fucking goose in Knockanilo,

or one hundred years later I'll forever wear this cheap smile
in a lay-by on Eglington Moor, spread on a filthy blanket
where my man is a guitar. He kneels on my legs and prays
that all our yellow hours may be eternal, and they are.

Or this one, wrapped in acres of brocade, nose bleeding,
my hands crossed in lace gloves, each finger ringed with jet,
a stoat fur stole draped across my shoulders, shaking
under a black mantilla. My eyes are lonely Durham tunnels.

Or here in my powder blue box suit with cream clutch bag
and auburn stockings and kitten-heeled shoes
where he has left me in scouring heat on a Pan American
World Airways flight to Buenos Aires that never even left.

History Lessons

Stepping out on silty summer platforms
under gastric soot and steam to parade:
party-goers, late-comers with carers,
crevice-jawed, uniformed, they seem so bad,
while we turn up in suits and hats to watch.

The station master waves and whistles
and our paraphernalia flakes off,
squints and sieves through its crammed-in ending.
The Crown Hotel is closed, its bunting gone.
The town square prepares its apology.

How quickly things disperse for the wretched,
just those Celias, Ethels and Mabels
clumped in front of the ironmongers now,
ready to greet each one they recognise.

War Games

You won't think of it as the presumption
of a hundred dawns, still less the boys
bringing it on with teeth like olive pits.

It can't be that column of soldiers you saw
dragging bouquets by a wood-tarred barn
hating the yards until what's fit to burst arrives.

If it's the yellow rind of Venus, sumptuous, pimply
as chicken skin, you can't believe that either.
When it runs – like a three-legged dog with

the face of Jesus – it won't be measured out
in cigarettes saying, 'Here it is, O here it is.'
And now, on the banged-up field, flopped with crows,

you feel cheated until red clouds, green clouds
disperse beneath the sometime stars; it
breeds again all that we need and makes us miss.

The Crabs

Trish says, 'I stopped drinking, son.'
'All the cute ones do,' I say. We smile and

it is after one on Myrtle Street. All day
the lead sky beats its way

over fire sales and crab packing yards
where the kids are dying.

A street of radios and weatherboard homes not worth spit.
'I may start over this evening.'

'I will join you in it,' I laugh. The creeps keep coming
to check on our yellow punished sofa.

We keep at it, volunteering through the small hours,
not drinking, inside our tiny purple shells.

It's Here Again

You're sitting by the tall lemon window,
your feet are scraping the Sarouk rug
while everything is seeping and shearing
through preposterous gardens. What do we see?

High bees putter and scat, the elms sag a little,
the least of today's light locks the foxglove angles
of the garden in a simple mouldy furnace;
somehow you are here and the songs of it reach

past all those tiny becomings into this puckered bat
that starts its clicking feast outside. Are we cheated?
When do ends start to fold and fret in poor weather?
Here then the counterpart of all ends flows fiercest

along the tart lane, along the broken pipes and paving,
through this hawthorn-draped, bell-decaying evening
with its thousand emerald icons. The smart blood sings,
Make haste, it sings, *Bring us wonder, bring rain.*

Anastasia in Crinolines

In those days, Vincenzo's letters arrived weekly.
Except for Beatrice, no one knew about the walks
inside our fussy orchard late at night. Beatrice
would join me often, smoking a pipe,
    talking of antelope or geese.

I felt weaker each day. Our meals consisted of cold veal,
loose cheese, slices of crisp white pear,
mushrooms simmered in thyme and tart Alsatian wine.
We felt deep sheaths of heat pour down
    from the Obermeyers' pine lodge.

Summer buzzards peeled free from pines and cried
inside the gorge. We loved to watch the cirrus
drift serenely through the glacial blue,
stowing hours we later named our 'English Empery',
    translating them.

I loved to see the garter snakes on goat paths
lying on the clay, beside a scattering of last year's
ash leaves, drifts of thorns, alcoves patched
with gaudy lichen, snakes obeying heat calls,
    needing me to know them.

Antonio returned in late September. All the birds
had changed, the skies were full of white storms,
heavy fruit in filthy baskets lined the parlour.
All the staff had left to winter by the lakes.
    Eduardo stacked the trunks

inside the hall but kept his counsel, sifting through
the house, he was another brittle shadow for me.
I learned new verbs. I learned the names of rivers,
bitter hills and valley towns and Turkish migrant roads
    along a goitered pass

and waited for Antonio to make his protestations.
Now no one came to visit. The only sound inside
each fostered evening was log fires seething,
cracking, whining, as we waited for advice of rooms
    in some Davos sanatorium.

Meeting at the Hayward
for Andrew Robinson

High up on that brutalist balcony
we leaned like city sparrows,
peering out across tiers of concrete
knocking back warm gallery wine
and loving London's gantries.

December '96, the Hodgkin show
that beefy old Sylvester hung
a few years from his end. I loved
its grey walls savaged with the ardour
in those works, the breaks outs

of citrine, emerald and vermilion,
yet we stepped away to talk about
the unseen seen, or memory and settlement
that's patterned in the paint, who knows?
Below us, blooming theatre signage

roused its galvanising news
that called on us to keep on being young
that winter – well, that is how I think of it –
escaped from all the others, seeing something
else that starts beyond the end of all the lights.

My Spell

All that sweats and tilts and cries,
all the stories in a drowning bed,
all that eats the minutes and hours,
and all the sweet bacon in this neighbourhood,
and the silent forests and far and near
the stewing birds, the pink star's song,
and the opera of your eyes tonight
by the home-going bridge and the grey rats leaving
and these charred walnuts and bitter grapes
and the gravy of this river,
all that attends my burrow tonight,
tonight where the winged god begs I beg,
his mouth the path to Tartarus.

Them Situationals

'I want to get back to when life mattered,'
is how Jimi started. 'How you fail is really
when the grace kicks in.'
                        I watch him bend
between pot plants, teasing ochre bedding
from the grey stacks, twisting in his rusted trowel
through lumps of clay. 'I hate to dwell on this.
It's over when you notice it; one day you're
in the middle, and then the middle ends.'
'Getting old,' I laugh.
                        'Yeah. Well, I ain't old yet.'
Jimi bends away and tucks his shirt tails
back into his pants. His corduroys are loose
on thick green suspenders. I see his hands are grey
and filthy with another hour of working.
'I ought to have expected it.' 'What's that?' I say.
'The ash of hope. Dis-inspiration's what I mean,
a calling ain't the same as making up a life.'
'Do you regret it? Wasting all them years lying
to yourself?'
                'It ain't lying if you do the work.
You gotta waste your days somehow, ain't you?'
He flashes me a glance beneath those heavy
brows and smiles. We laugh a little then.
'It mostly doesn't matter what you do,
or how hard you do it. When your grandmother
was alive, God bless her, we would drive out
fast from here, make out in the woods, rinse off
in the east river back of Ron Shaughnessy's place,
and later, count some stars; we never knew

their names. I think I learned a lot back then,
about those common joys, what I like to call
the situationals. The things we don't just live among,
but in, the life inside the things we see.
This being in it is the most important thing
for us. Heck, time don't matter much. That happens
anyways. How much of it, how little, you know,
that stuff is all distraction. There's a tiny space
inside the world for you to sort of occupy.
But there's a lot of framing too. You gotta see past
all the framing to the essence of your task.
That sort of work don't get much notice.
You won't get no mentions or no bylines
in the dailies, nothing like that. It ain't about
them fashions for the complex points or them
fashions for the simplest line of thinking
anyone can muster. Saying something easy
ain't a virtue – no how, no way. But saying
what is hard in one way fully graspable,
but not fully comprehensible, that's tough,
and it won't win you friends, no plaudits neither,
or money down at Ron's for a shot of whiskey.'

Jimi stops to rub his back, he turns to look at me.
'Them situationals is what you've got to work on.
The rest of it is dirt.'
                      Then he gets back to things,
pressing in the trowel, picking out the dead leaves
from the seeds that seem to matter.

A Bouquet

I put you in this song
where dry flower-heads split, where
night seeds and plush November stoats
    sew a line through the barley.

And I ache for you entirely
without my spells and loanwords for
moon-anchor, bittern-drum,
    alone-in-the-lane.

Here I tighten all the strings
and bow out the smallest tune
to our cider-bright night
    and all the crushed roses.

Tidelines

I know we're there on the frayed road east
    lost in the last estate to love in –
Slackcote or Sholver or Linfitts
    where your choices end but life begins.

Mouthless terracing, fly-tipped ridges
    before a fringe of oaks and birches.
Each town tears free another year,
    the city's shore begins to clear.

A Town Called 'Proverbs'

I teach you proverbs by puce stone steps,
cracking cedars lift away, paradisal birds are free,
our eyes cannot see the fossilised coyote.
Our deep valley turns perpetual. Evening reels
and we link arms on the incomplete street.

A tiny man is serving pastelillos of hot sweet beef
and everything subsumes itself. The phantom city dazzles
with high rouge glass. We are surely fleeing Earth
and our gassy route is cheap. We brood on the bypass
where interstitial apartments hide the moon each night.

Nothing can be moved without ropes of sorrow.
Nothing may be left without a bird in the heart.
She who will lead you must be changed by bells.
The perfect life is served with tomorrow's tears.
A field for your heart but a valley for love.

Identity

But what is left is what is bothering me.
Whose debt, what's torn, who departs from me
to bring up this fuss I leave behind
on wheat-coloured ruts where a farm
exempts each life. I visit this in long
January darkness that divides all colour
to bring no self nor the self's shadow.
If you imagine it whole, the ghost is burned.

But that's it really, the cold parish winter
thoughts make on the leaking land I love.
Where I call to you to come back once
to let me ask this final sort of question
I can't quite form but know I need of you.
It makes me wonder how I learned
to be alone inside a feast of clocks;
the lies it took to now be solely you.

Goodbye, Gifford

The terracotta aprons of your soil
are home to industrial crows,
the spare ghost of air limns the ochre roofs.
Whitewash and lung-drift of wood smoke.
Autumn's rusty lime trees
smooching along beside the bleach field
and clipped paddocks of heritage.

Goodbye, Gifford. Goodbye.
The small exotic of your green blush
rushing the scouring path by the old waters –
the swinging burn's rattle and small drink.
Your cattle epoch and Laird's small parading glance.
Yester Parish Church's cone of God
latching onto a grave's kneeling carbon
reverence at the road junction.

And either silence or dog barks, it seems.
Yester House lies like a repertory set,
real as opera, as out of town, out of life.
The flavours of wind soothing our veins
amid apoplectic leaf-fall, and now
the tree-storm's upturned house of roots.
The sybaritic mist. Palace of gravitas.
Guerdon. Late field-gasp. Fox-burr.

Goodbye, Gifford. As your clocks parade
their small furies, we can't walk from here
through bees and mild widows,
as flowers sign their small delicious fevers.

You're spoor-shifting in the growing emblems
of lime-mist. We can stroll awhile,
marking our distance in the coming
together of things. Sorting old brilliance
as wood smoke stirs the dream-bill
of a heron's twilit, aberrant flight.

The Herald

He said it must have been a reckoning hand
that fell upon the valley, God's hand maybe
pushed its weight about the pigs and runts
where winterlight and stale gold planets framed
unchosen cliff-falls. The mad land leapt, miles of it
shaking free what the outdated maps
had meant. It was a queer penance or admission
no one stood for. Our dreams fell in the sea.
What was left was just eternity. As if
this spreading waste was empty of the things it took.
And as we blinked at him, growing bored
of all his earnestness, the path broke free
and quiet tons of yellow clay and chalk
softly took him too, his life one step away
from bearing this hard news and being it.

Fresh Deliveries
i.m. Brendan Kennelly

In that red cream thaw tomorrow morning
we shall each drink in whatever sun we can
and make it through the short fog of the farm
like autumn calves, the half-made heirs
that come to stand in glaucous mud
      by the steel gate there.

We shall all be unnamed regulars, wet nosed
as light draws through its final grey
fingers at five a.m., sorting the first available crows,
the first available cobs and then, as it lifts,
a smitten road where the post van comes
      with news of our death.

Under the Mesas

Your red dog life in the ward
bearing phantom wounds like a palomino
and, yes, you should listen to these cowboy songs:
haberdasheries, wood towns, peach dawns.
The hell of horses kicking in the breeze.
Valleys failing like limbs far, far from the chaparral.

You tucked in your wallet on the lonesome plain
and screwed your life into a ball.
Whatever gave out, brought no twisted auburn river
under mesas. No one raised a fist to this,
no one yawned over burlap or ten-gallon hats,
or even wore chaps. You kissed the rangy stars
and fell from heaven like a goldfinch – boom!

This is a desperate county that
someone has filled with tiny people.
We are counting, we keep counting them
riding south to the wide and useless border
on the sweet yawl of God's hot land. It bends away
in rhinestones and ringlets and never ends.

Ring All the Bells

And when January dies you watch
all its smoky light and dead ends
peel away from you outside
a granite township of bells and gulls.

And there's that coughing lift-off
when you realise you have survived
its bitumen-soaked oakum once again.

I hope the endless month takes with it
everything including
this slow savage harbour
with a thousand stickmen
carrying shears, cutting sails
from all the felt ships, the grey hulks stowing
hideous chests of winter teeth.

I want anchors to twist free, ropes to coil up.
I want a boatswain to scream time
for the great departure.
I want each ship to be the last I ever see
swaying off the anthracite coast,
taking dead brains to their final colony.

Minor Comedy

I want to make it to the air-free cold denuded top
like major poets do.
The ones who never seem to stop.
The ones we wait for in a smelly Southbank queue.
The ones with rakish friends that sing false perpetual praises
and meet at gigs in castles in unpronounceable Middle-
    European places.

I want the jam, the cake, the cream,
I want the whole slim volume dream.
I want the prizes and the money.
I want the campus-rooted, lecture-touring,
student-clustered, whole American foundation scoring
land of odes and honey.

I want a 'Time to Write' grant from the mandarins at ACE.
I want to be the first poet in space.
I want to stare back from pinkish clouds Olympian
over drunken decades of small magazine oblivion
that led here to my godhead, freshly featured in *Time Out*.
The Laureate's Laureate, the kid with clout.

And I want better rhymes than these,
or no rhymes at all, for academics in long essays to
    ecstatically tease
hot meanings into rapture. And I want, with all our golden
    multitudes, to *please*.
In major television interviews to gaze and nod and lap up
    wild applause.

I want to cause a change in several wicked international laws.
I want a thin grey spouse who plays Satie well in a swanky
 tower block in Espoo.
I want a bristling dramaturge for an affair in Timbuktu.
I want to hear my words falling like manna, heaven sent,
on the black-robed lemon-sucking North London
 establishment.

Yet I never want to write [successfully] in semi-comic verse
that which may reveal the whiffy bilge tank of pique,
or worse
an inconsistent compositional technique.

Naturally, I'll heartily propose I want the very same for you
in every farmhouse masterclass I run in Devon-scented glory.
Late at night, with slippers propped and a tinkling whisky
 sour,
in my dark electric hour alone, I'll watch the star shelf pour
nightmares through my hopeless story.

How Small We Were

How small we were in the cheap afternoon
where all the pennies are old: the bad tennis,
each dreary weekend with its clip earrings,
raw hands, loose kisses, food wet with decay.
Where the great friends cheered from a dance hall
each bruised sun, vinegar sea, lidless moon.
Regal adventures worn above the rats
as the rats chased their hurrying evening.
We knew each closing church was a cake tin,
filled with our chintzy marriage payload.
Us like newsprint found beneath the carpet
that holds our silly decades column neat.
We hold on, we keep holding on, while rain
tanks the precinct and the roads run out.

Jackson's Brick Works

Except we didn't know it then,
yelping on high bits, dead legging,
racing by a grease-slow brook
then jumping, coats off, landing,
snorting with the shock of it
ankle-deep in stew-soft mud
leaving two pathetic mouths
to close behind in the clay
and by the swilling bank spy
erratic solemn weeds,
a rat's cobble that moved,
and beyond our screams
the pretence of a hill fort
whose lost foundations
no one could name.

Jackson's brick works, Hale Lane.
Caught between schools
we'd dig out broken
tobacco pipes from Failsworth tip
to scrutinise the fossil
each presented: a featureless
face, a smooth cup
you imagined cupped
in someone else's mucky paws,
pressing in sweet threads
from a pocket pouch, sucking
in soft clucks, pausing, sucking,
nodding to the others who
later would be lost, and no one
ever named.

The Comeuppance

He took the stolen bushel, the hand-off neat.
Soanes, soot-beleaguered, hides in the cellar, beat.
The pastry-coloured pantry teems with shadows.
The scullery swells with heat. Candle ends are smoking.

Now Baines steps forward from the safe room
in his soda-stained waistcoat, his brisket face rigid,
to announce the silverware's gone swimmingly.
Magnolia dreams and cartilage hours. Noon distends.
Field rats move through silent stooks. Fish is broiled.

At three, the rozzers whisk in with that old toff, Herbert,
to search the boot room. Ratcliffe talked. They find
the stash.
        Ten months later, toothless Soanes is back
to flop inside the staff house with his hands all nubbed, but
for that year he straightens up the Orangery, digs a ha-ha,
cuts back wild hydrangeas till his guts pack in.

Standing by his graveside, the service over, his winter family
senses what? A burning field? Magpies strutting
where the sun rubs out its gormless scarlet?
                                    His son lights up.
Rooks settle by a chisel moon. The coffin cart moves off.

Folk Tale

That with stoats pulled such tunes in a green well
and made loose an axe, walled snow, exile, sea.

And danced and held arms out with our black joy
and cracked stones with boots where the birds all fell.

Come now, through November's fires that lovers
find fern-relaxed, rain-raked and tall with smoke,

you will not make church music here, daughter.
No one may bargain for the shadow hare.

No one may scrape lust light with an oak heart.
No one judge the stock of a blind house.

At this point along the shingle beach
she will pick up a canter and bare teeth

and set a blood watch for the sweetest men.
That's our promise and we are coming now.

My Idea of Heaven

What if light is formed from time
and time is light, an arrow of it always
transiting the tiny lives of stars,
and even when stars die, those histories
travelling ferocious cold,
passing total distance as if nothing
knocked the dark sea that cannot end –
would our deaths yet be a coming child
ferrying new cries with all the others,
the light still vigorous with each of us?

Acknowledgements

I'm sincerely grateful to Rishi Dastidar and Rory Waterman for their kind words about this collection.

Thanks are also due to the editors of the following magazines where some of these poems first appeared, often in different forms:

14 Magazine
Cambridge Poetry Magazine
The Clearing
Cōnfingō Magazine
Fenland Poetry Journal
Ink, Sweat & Tears
Littoral Magazine

The London Magazine
The Moth
New Welsh Review
Northampton Poetry Review
PN Review
Stride Magazine

'The Statue' was first published in *Sculpted: Poetry of the North West*, edited by Lindsey Holland and Angela Topping. Thank you to the editors.

This book has been typeset by
SALT PUBLISHING LIMITED
using Sabon, a font designed by Jan Tschichold
for the D. Stempel AG, Linotype and Monotype
Foundries. It has been manufactured using Holmen
Book Cream 65gsm paper, and printed and bound by
Clays Limited in Bungay, Suffolk, Great Britain.

CROMER
GREAT BRITAIN
MMXXV